# New England

# New England

## John S Bowman

**LONGMEADOW PRESS**
A Bison Book

*This edition produced exclusively for Longmeadow Press by*

Bison Books Corp.
17 Sherwood Place
Greenwich, CT 06830

ISBN 0-681-40041-2

Printed in Hong Kong

*Page: 1:* An idyllic farm setting in
Tunbridge, Vermont, in autumn.
*Pages 2-3:* A harbor sunset in
Boothbay, Maine.
*This page:* Sheep graze on a
hillside with a colorful foliage
backdrop near Pawlett, Vermont.

## Acknowledgments

The author and publisher would like to thank the following people who have helped in
the preparation of this book: Mary R Raho, who did the photo research; Mike Rose, who
designed it; Barbara Thrasher, who edited it.

## Picture Credits

Marcello Bertinetti: 14 bottom left, 15 top, 21 both, 23 top, 84 bottom right, 88 bottom, 90
John Calabrese: 42-43 bottom
State of Connecticut photograph: 40-41, 43 right, 45 top, 46 top, 49 top left, right and
  bottom right
Dartmouth College, Hanover, New Hampshire: 62 bottom
FPG/International: (R. Harris) 6-7, (Nichols) 12-13, (J Blank) 14 bottom right, 15 bottom,
  80-81, (A D'Amario) 18 right, (W Wilson) 24 top, (J Viesti) 25 bottom, (Taylor) 32 top,
  33, (J Hailey) 42 left, (F Dole) 46 bottom, (Hallinan) 24 bottom left, 50-51,
  (T McCarthy) 54 bottom right, (R Thomas) 55, (Sigl) 59 top, (Wendler) 60-61,
  (N Graffman) 62 top right, (Ahrens) 63, (H Ross) 66-67, (P Boisvert) 68 top, 72-73,
  (C Smith) 69, 70-71, (J Randklev) 75 top, (F Dole) 92-93, (E Nagele) 94-95, 96
John Foraste, Brown University: 34 top, 35
Jeff Gnass: 16-17, 19, 28-29, 58, 74, 89
Janine M Katsigianis: 84 bottom left
John Katsigianis: 62 top left, 75 bottom
M A C Miles: 24 bottom right
New Hampshire Office of Visitors and Tourism: 54 bottom left
Rhode Island Department of Tourism: 31 top, 32 bottom, 37 top
H Armstrong Roberts: 10-11, 14 top, 18 bottom left, (Burgess) 20, (J Blank) 22, 23
  bottom, ( F Sieb) 25 top, 26-27, 30, 31 bottom, J Blank 38-39, 44, (J Urwiller) 46-47,
  (R Krubner) 48, (J Blank) 52-53, (Avis) 54 top, 64-65, (M Schreiders) 78-79,
  (H Abernathy) 84 top right, (J Irwin) 85, 86, (L George) 89 top, A Griffith) 91
Jerry Sieve: 2-3, 4-5, 56-57, 82-83, 87
Strawbery Banke, Portsmouth, NH: 59 below
Sugarbush Valley, Warren, VT: 68 bottom
Mike Tamborrino: 18 top left
Barry Tenin: 34 bottom, 36 all, 37 bottom, 45 bottom
State of Vermont ADCA: 1, 9, 71 right, 76-77
Angela White: 84 top left

# Contents

Massachusetts 11

Rhode Island 27

Connecticut 39

New Hampshire 51

Vermont 64

Maine 81

# Introduction

New England! It's very name pays tribute to its unique historical origins, and reflects a cultural and geographic region that embraces both past and present. Some parts of the country have longer histories than does New England (even though New Englanders tend to ignore this): the South and the Southwest can point to Spanish roots that go considerably farther back than the British origins of New England, while Virginia can claim even older English roots than its sister states to the north. But New England's name embodies two particular dimensions of its distinctive history: the strong sense of its Old World ties and the consciousness of having evolved from that older culture into new modes of thinking and being. It is this history, this sense of itself, that still colors New England, that makes it what a non-native, Bernard de Voto, called 'a finished place.'

New England, de Voto went on to say, 'is the first American section to be finished, to achieve stability in the conditions of its life. It is the first . . . permanent civilization in America.' Contemporary Americans, as a whole, might demur slightly at that 'permanent civilization,' and today's New Englanders would probably deny that they have achieved quite such stability. But New England maintains a distinctive sense of place in its old mills, its winding country roads, its stone walls snaking through hilly forests, its wealth of historic landmarks, its busy harbors and its buildings. At the same time, there is a unique dynamic to contemporary New England — even if photographers traditionally tend to focus on the old stabilities. The region's population is now as diverse as that of any part of the United States: long gone are the days when New England was populated mostly by 'old Yankees.' There is a diverse economy these days, too — one dependent no longer on maritime commerce and manufacturing, not only on farms and time-honored crafts but on the latest technology and the arts. Certainly no one needs to be reminded about the diversity of New England's weather: the illustrations that follow reflect the realities of the four seasons. And the architecture reflects a corresponding diversity: any major New England city reveals the juxtaposition of the old and the new. The name remains the strongest clue to the character of the region.

New England was founded by men and women who were determined to start a new society, and their enduring exertions inspire the visitor, the historian, and the roving photographer: the graceful spired churches in which early New Englanders chose to work out new ways of relating to God; the spare but beautiful utopian communities like those of the Shakers, whose whole way of life expressed their belief that it was 'a gift to be simple'; the various state houses that asserted a free people's rights with increasing confidence and effectiveness. Side by side with these New World developments are the many replicas of the Old World — the fine houses and stately public buildings still found throughout the region (and, in many cases, still lived in and utilized). In this apparent paradox — that New Englanders wanted something both new and old — lies, perhaps, the deepest insight into the region and its people.

Sunset at Bass Harbor, Maine.

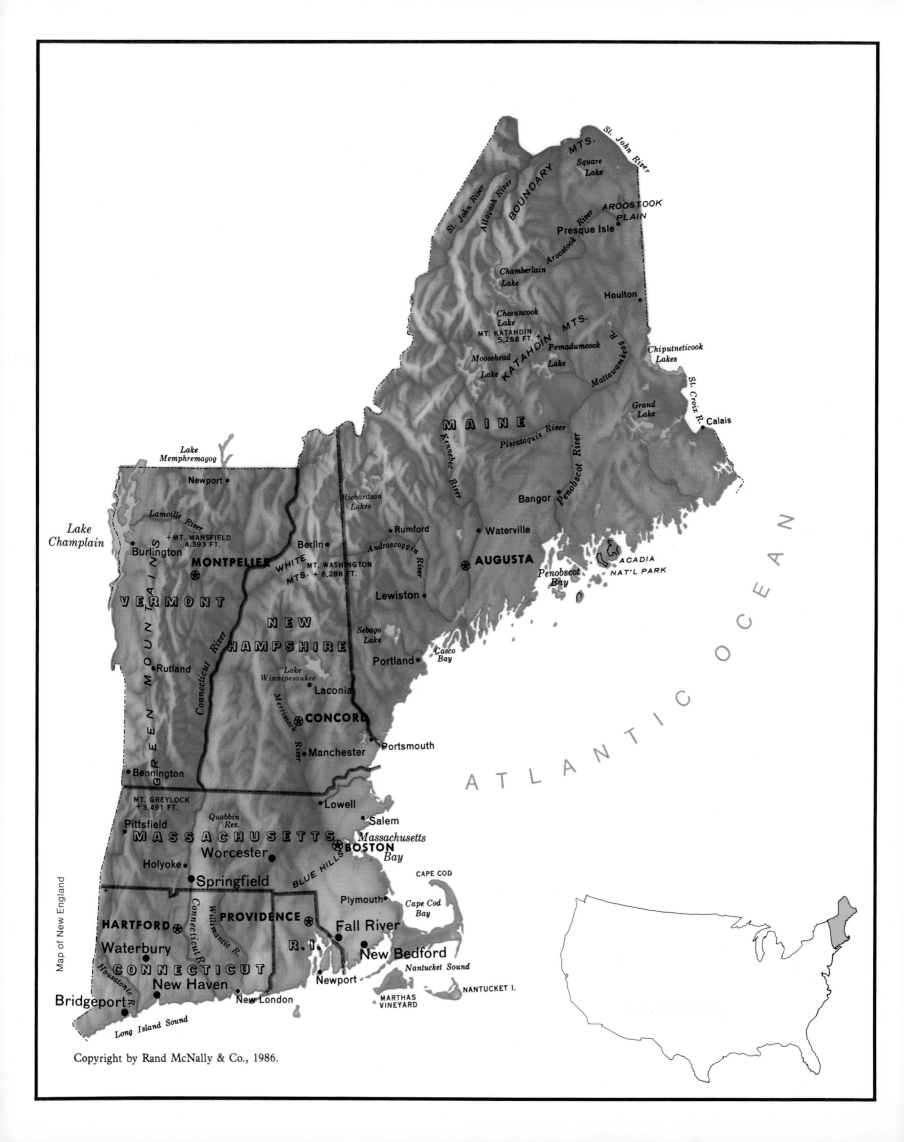

Map of New England

BOUNDARY MTS.

St. John River

Square Lake

St. John River

Allagash River

AROOSTOOK PLAIN

Presque Isle

Aroostook River

Chamberlain Lake

Houlton

Chesuncook Lake

MT. KATAHDIN 5,268 FT. +

KATAHDIN MTS.

Pemadumcook Lake

Moosehead Lake

Mattawamkeag R.

Chiputneticook Lakes

MAINE

Piscataquis River

Grand Lake

St. Croix R.

Calais

Lake Memphremagog

Kennebec River

Penobscot River

Newport

Richardson Lakes

Bangor

Waterville

Lamoille River

Rumford

Berlin

Androscoggin River

ACADIA NAT'L PARK

Lake Champlain

+ MT. MANSFIELD 4,393 FT.

AUGUSTA

Burlington

MONTPELIER

WHITE MTS. + MT. WASHINGTON 6,288 FT.

Lewiston

Penobscot Bay

VERMONT

NEW HAMPSHIRE

Sebago Lake

ATLANTIC OCEAN

Connecticut River

Portland

Casco Bay

GREEN MOUNTAINS

Rutland

Lake Winnipesaukee

Laconia

Merrimack River

CONCORD

Bennington

Manchester

Portsmouth

MT. GREYLOCK + 3,491 FT.

Lowell

Quabbin Res.

Salem

Pittsfield

MASSACHUSETTS

Massachusetts Bay

Worcester

BOSTON

Holyoke

BLUE HILLS

CAPE COD

Springfield

Plymouth

Cape Cod Bay

HARTFORD

PROVIDENCE

Willimantic R.

Connecticut R.

R.I.

Fall River

Waterbury

CONNECTICUT

New Bedford

Nantucket Sound

Housatonic R.

New Haven

Newport

NANTUCKET I.

Bridgeport

New London

MARTHAS VINEYARD

Long Island Sound

Copyright by Rand McNally & Co., 1986.

A field strewn with dandelions beside a country road in Waitsfield, Vermont.

# Massachusetts

# Massachusetts

Massachusetts was the first place in New England to support a permanent colony of Europeans. Certainly it is not first by virtue of size — three other New England states, in fact, are larger, and indeed there are only five American states that are smaller in area. The population of Massachusetts, however, lifts it to tenth place among the 50 states, and this in turn says something about the intensity of life in this relatively small area. For all these people over all these years have inevitably produced much history and culture and left their imprints on the land.

For history, there is, to begin with, Plymouth Rock and Plimoth Plantation: most New Englanders choose to forget the earlier settlements in Virginia — let alone the Spanish in the Southwest. (Alternatively, they like to think that Leif Ericson may have explored the New England coast about AD 1000.) Ten years after the Pilgrims founded Plymouth, another group of English Protestants, the Puritans, seeking a place to worship in freedom, settled on Masschusetts Bay and founded Boston. In the decades that followed, the settlers of Massachusetts brought many of the accoutrements of European culture to their land — not only the houses and public buildings, the furniture and artifacts, the mills, barns and shipyards, but newspapers, libraries and schools. Massachusetts would lay claim to many educational milestones: the first secondary school (Boston Latin, 1635), the first college (Harvard, 1636), the first public high school (Boston English, 1821), the first college for women (Mount Holyoke, 1837). Massachusetts might arguably claim to have been the breeding ground of the American Revolution, whether it be traced to the Boston Tea Party of 1773 or to the battles at Lexington and Concord in April 1775.

In the end, though, those who know and love Massachusetts best will be the first to insist that their Commonwealth (one of four such within the United States) is far more than a history lesson. It is a coastal land at one end, and less than 200 miles to the west it is a mountainous land. The area between includes progressive cities, scenic towns, prosperous farms and unspoiled forests.

*Preceding page:* At Rockport's picturesque old harbor on Cape Ann, sunset envelops boats at anchor around Motif No. 1, the fishermen's shack painted by many artists.

*Left:* This replica of the gristmill built by early settler John Jenney in 1636 at Plymouth grinds grain with waterpower as did the original.

*Opposite top:* Standing in front of the monumental entrance to the Boston Museum of Fine Arts, which opened in 1905, is the bronze statue, 'Appeal to the Great Spirit,' created by the American sculptor, Cyrus Dallin, in 1908.

*Opposite far left:* Buildings typical of Boston's Back Bay line Commonwealth Avenue, the main thoroughfare of this section, built literally on filled land in the old bay during the nineteenth century. Tree-shaded Commonwealth Avenue was inspired by the boulevards of Paris; many of its fine houses are now divided into apartments.

*Opposite near left:* Boston's old Haymarket Square, once the site of a hay market, has for many years now been taken over by modern buildings and highways, but street merchants still sell their goods here.

*Top:* Restored Quincy Market with its many shops and restaurants has become a popular tourist attraction.

*Right:* The center section of the State House of Massachusetts was designed by Charles Bulfinch, the first professional American architect; it was erected between 1795 and 1798. With its dome — gilded in the nineteenth century — it is in the classic revival style.

*Preceding pages:* Boston's modern skyline reflects the setting sun of an October day, as viewed from the Cambridge side of the Charles River. The old Back Bay is in the foreground.

*Left top:* This whale serves as a weathervane on the steeple of a church in New Bedford — an appropriate symbol for the city that was once the whaling capital of America.

*Left:* The bronze statue by Leonard Craske, 'The Gloucester Fisherman,' gazes out to sea from America's first fishing port and seems impervious, as in real life, to the weather.

*Above:* The battleship *USS Massachusetts* is one of several former US Navy ships on public display in Fall River. Commissioned in 1942, the battleship saw action in the European and Pacific theaters in World War II. Decommissioned, she was brought to Fall River in 1965 as the state's memorial to its dead in World War II.

*Opposite:* The frigate *USS Constitution,* 'Old Ironsides,' is docked at Boston's Charleston Navy Yard. Built between 1794 and 1797, she fought against the Tripoli pirates and in the War of 1812.

*Above:* The cranberry bog is typical of the coastal region of southeastern Massachusetts, where half the nation's cranberry crop is grown. The cranberry vine thrives in marshy areas and sandy bogs, which are deliberately flooded to protect plants from temperature extremes or drought.

*Opposite above:* A pleasure boat cruises through the Cape Cod Canal. Massachusetts' numerous inlets, estuaries, bays and small rivers allow many of the inhabitants of its eastern region to maintain boats of all kinds to enjoy the summer months at sea.

*Opposite below:* This old house, with its cedar shingles, is typical of the fine homes found at Siasconset, on Nantucket Island, some 30 miles south of Cape Cod. Long ago an important center of whaling and maritime trade, now Nantucket is popular as a vacation retreat.

*Left:* The harbor of the old fishing village of Menemsha, on Martha's Vineyard. A major whaling center in the eighteenth century, the island of Martha's Vineyard is now a quiet refuge for summer visitors.

*Above:* Cape Cod is a great 'flexed' arm that extends off the southern coast of Massachusetts — at its narrowest, barely two miles wide, so that, as here at North Truro, the inner bay seems separated from the Atlantic Ocean by only a strip of sand. The Cape Cod National Seashore now makes much of this outer stretch of the Cape a public preserve.

*Right:* At Eastham, in the central part of Cape Cod, stands the old grist windmill; dating from at least late eighteenth century, it was totally restored in the 1930s.

*Right:* The white, spired church standing on the edge of the town green is probably the most characteristic image of New England. This one is the Congregational Church in Williamstown, in the northwestern corner of the state. Williamstown is widely known as the home of Williams College, founded in 1793.

*Below:* The Minuteman Statue in Lexington, sculpted by Henry Kitson, commemorates the rebellious colonists' stand against the British on 18 April 1775, an action also immortalized in Henry Wadsworth Longfellow's epic poem, 'The Midnight Ride of Paul Revere.'

*Below right:* As elsewhere throughout America, the annual Fourth of July parade marches down the main street of Pittsfield, county seat and largest city in the Berkshires, the western region of Massachusetts. Pittsfield still maintains much of the atmosphere of a New England small town although it is in fact the hometown of part of General Electric.

*Above:* The Dwight-Barnard House, dated to about 1725, is one of many eighteenth and early-nineteenth century houses and public buildings that have either survived in or been moved to the mile-long main street that now makes up Historic Deerfield. (The Dwight-Barnard House was moved here in 1950 from Springfield, some 30 miles to the south.) The real old Deerfield was virtually destroyed twice in wars with the Indians (in 1675 and 1704), but it was resettled and in the twentieth century turned into a 'living museum.'

*Right:* The striking Round Stone Barn was built by the Shakers in 1826 at one of their most prosperous settlements, Hancock Village, just west of Pittsfield. The Shakers, a utopian sect who were found throughout the Northeast in the nineteenth century, stressed utility in their designs.

# Rhode Island

# Rhode Island

Until recently, every schoolchild knew at least one fact about Rhode Island: it has the smallest area of all the 50 United States. Now, thanks to the popularity of trivia games, almost everyone knows a second fact: it has the longest name of all the states. For the offical name is State of Rhode Island and Providence Plantation. This name contains within it the seeds of the state's history, a history characterized by the interaction of two separate regions — a maritime culture comprising three dozen islands and centered in Newport and a land-based economy centered in Providence.

Rhode Island itself received its name from one of two sources, depending on which historians are emphasizing which evidence. One school holds that it was named *Roadt Eylandt* — 'red island' in Dutch — in 1614 by the Dutch navigator Adriaen Block, because of red clay found there. Another school holds that it was named by European sailors who noticed its shape was similar to that of the island of Rhodes in the Mediterranean. However it got its name, this is the largest of the 36 islands that now make up the state, most of them situated in or around the Narragansett Bay, which covers about 20 percent of the state's land area and effectively cuts it into two unequal sections. The state's other well known island is Block Island, some nine miles off the southern tip of the state.

This great bay, then, and its attendant islands, all but guaranteed that the state would develop as a maritime economy, as indeed it did. Starting in the 1600s, shipyards along the bay built hundreds of ships for commerce and fishing; Rhode Islanders would take the lead in organizing the new navy for the American Revolution; and in our own day Rhode Island has the US Naval War College as well as one of the leading oceanographic research centers, the University of Rhode Island's, at Saunderstown.

Meanwhile, the 'plantation' economy was developing on the mainland, and now some 85 percent of the state's population live in an almost continuous metropolitan region from Pawtucket through Providence to Warwick. Although agriculture was the basis of the early economy, Rhode Islanders were quick to turn to the new ways of industry, so that the state now has a highly diversified economy, just as it boasts of a heterogeneous population. Islands and mainland, Providence and Newport, colonists and immigrants — little Rhode Island has it all.

*Preceding pages:* The statue of Roger Williams, founder of Providence in 1636, gazes over the center of the city from Prospect Terrace.

*Left:* A typical Rhode Island farm bathed in the light of an October afternoon. This farm, known as 'Little Rest' till 1885, is in Kingston.

*Left:* The State House of Rhode Island is built of white Georgia marble and in the Early Republican style. Designed by McKim, Mead and White, it was begun in 1895 and the General Assembly first met here in 1901.
*Above:* The John Brown House in Providence was designed by his brother Joseph, one of four brothers who contributed much to eighteenth century Rhode Island. Built between 1786 and 1788, the house was regarded by John Quincy Adams as the most magnificent in North America.

*Below:* The Old Slater Mill on the Seekonk River in Pawtucket is the oldest truly successful textile mill in the USA. It was built by Samuel Slater, who immigrated here in 1790 and introduced English manufacturing techniques.

*Above:* The Ocean Drive and Cliff Walk, now open to the public, were once the exclusive property of the wealthy elite who constructed their summer 'cottages' here in Newport after the Civil War.

*Below:* Dominating the point at Newport, with Cliff Walk in the foreground, is The Breakers, the most elaborate of the great mansions. Built by Cornelius Vanderbilt in the 1890s for over $3 million, it was designed by Richard M Hunt in a pseudo-Renaissance style that employs much marble, carved stone and mosaics.

*Right:* Cattle graze in a field in Middletown, once the northern section of Newport which became independent in 1743, realizing it had little in common with urban Newport.

*Top:* These people are engaging in one of the oldest and still favorite occupations of all who come to Rhode Island — digging for clams. For the best 'clamming,' people wait till the tide is out and then venture onto the flats to dig with special rakes or hoes. Both soft and hard-shell clams are taken from the shores. The hard-shell clams were called *quahogs* by the Indians, who used them as *wampum*, or money.

*Above:* Men sort out a sizable haul of fish at dockside.

*Right:* This small boat rides at rest in one of the countless inlets that line the shores of Rhode Island; with its many islands, inlets and bays, Rhode Island claims some 390 miles of coastline.

*Top:* One of the major diversions that Rhode Island offers is fishing. The ports of the state once hosted large commercial fishing fleets; these have declined, but sport fishing remains popular.
*Above:* Visitors and natives agree that nothing tastes quite like food and drink at one of the many dockside restaurants that line the shores of Rhode Island.
*Right:* Sailing and yachting are favorite diversions offered by Rhode Island. For over a century American yachtsmen defended the America's Cup in the waters off Newport.
*Opposite top:* A more recent attraction in Rhode Island is the sport of ballooning.
*Opposite bottom:* Rhode Island's shore offers many miles of fine beaches for swimming and sunbathing. People from all over southern New England flock to them in the summer.

# Connecticut

Although it is conventional to call many states 'a place of contrasts' perhaps none deserves it more than Connecticut: even two of its nicknames — Constitution State and Provision State — embody polarities. For Connecticut's long history has always tended to embrace these two dimensions — the idealistic aspirations signified by the white, spired village church on the green, and the hardheaded Yankee practicalities signified by the helicopter and nuclear-submarine manufacturers. Visitors and natives have come to appreciate them both.

Connecticut's polarization began shortly after the first colonists, English settlers from Massachusetts, moved into Windsor in 1633. (The Dutch had, in fact, built a fort on the site of Hartford a year earlier, but they never made a permanent settlement.) Many of these early English settlers had left Massachusetts to obtain more religious and political freedom, and in 1639 the Connecticut Colony (which united settlements at Windsor, Hartford and Wethersfield) adopted the Fundamental Orders, which set down the right of voters to elect their own government officials — in effect a written constitution. As time went on this high idealism of the early decades was matched by the colonists' industry: by the early 1700s Connecticut was becoming known for its shipbuilding, silversmithing and clockmaking. Connecticut's itinerant salesmen carried the colony's products throughout the other colonies, becoming the prototype of the shrewd Yankee peddlers. It was the colony's readiness to supply so much food, clothing and other necessities to the Continental Army during the Revolution that led George Washington to dub Connecticut 'the Provision State.'

The state's other nickname came from the Constitutional Convention in Philadelphia in 1787, which threatened to come apart over the issue of delegates to Congress: the large states wanted the number based on population, the smaller states wanted the same number for all states. It was Connecticut's Roger Sherman who proposed the compromise that produced both the two-tier Congress and the sobriquet 'The Constitution State.'

During the nineteenth century, the pendulum seemed to swing the other way, as Connecticut took the lead in many new inventions and industries: it was no coincidence that one of its adopted sons placed a 'Connecticut Yankee' in King Arthur's court. And to this day, both tendencies, the practical and the idealistic, tend to find expression in Connecticut's energetic cities and tranquil hills and river valleys.

*Preceding pages:* The pleasure boats and private residences that have taken over this harbor at Westport are typical of Connecticut's new coastal 'image.'

*Left:* A garden supply store operates out of one of the fine old buildings that survive in Wethersfield, an early English settlement south of Hartford.

*Left above:* Snow covers a cornfield. Some of New England's most fertile land can be found in the Connecticut River Valley, which stretches all the way from Long Island Sound north through Connecticut, through western Massachusetts and to Canada, dividing Vermont and New Hampshire.

*Left:* A summer scene on the edge of Bridgeport, now the largest city in Connecticut. Like virtually all American states, Connecticut's original occupation was farming. Bridgeport, at the mouth of the Pequonnock River on Long Island Sound, began as a whaling port, then moved into industry by the mid-nineteenth century to become the center of early manufacturing.

*Above:* A dairy farm — as indicated by its silo filled with fodder for the cattle over the winter — hibernates in the cold and snow. Connecticut still supports a thriving dairy industry — now including goats as well as cows — on its gently rolling land and fertile pastures.

*Far left:* Marigolds, petunias and roses front a picket fence while colorful lobster buoys decorate the weathered shingles of a typical New England house in Groton Long Point, located in eastern Connecticut on Long Island Sound. Nearby Fishers Island, a couple of miles offshore is a popular resort community where boating and fishing are favorite summertime activities.

*Opposite:* The capitol of Connecticut overlooks Hartford from Capitol Hill. Designed by the notable nineteenth-century American architect Richard Upjohn, it was erected in 1878 and replaced the more modest old State House (a work of Charles Bulfinch from 1798). This Capitol is in the Gothic Revival style, although its eclecticism and exuberance take it outside any simple historical architectural style. The 12-sided gilded dome is topped by a winged figure representing 'the Genius of Connecticut,' by Randolph Rogers.

*Above:* The final glow of sunset gives way to the lights of Hartford's modern skyscrapers that now dominate the center city. The Dutch first settled here in 1633, followed in 1635 by the English, who pushed the Dutch out by 1654. Maritime commerce in the eighteenth century and industry in the nineteenth century made the city prosperous, but it is as 'The Insurance Capital of America' that Hartford is now known. Its companies began with maritime insurance in the eighteenth century, then moved into fire insurance in the nineteenth century and gained the reputation for prompt payments that secured its future.

*Right:* The fast-growing city of Stamford, in Fairfield County, is divided by Route I-95, and is now the home of many businesses which have moved out of New York City.

*Above:* The fishing docks at Stonington, a quiet old town at the easternmost point of the state, right at the border with Rhode Island. Once known as 'the Nursery for Seamen,' Stonington was a center of shipbuilding, merchant and whaling fleets, and of master seamen well into the nineteenth century, when Federal funds were allotted to build a protective breakwater. After the Civil War, with the emergence of steamships, the port lost its importance. Some fishermen still put out to sea from here, but Stonington is now best known as a refuge for more urban Northeasterners who prize the beauty and solitude it offers.

*Right:* The town of Mystic is located on the tidal outlet of the Mystic River in northeastern Connecticut. An old port for fisherman and commercial ships, it was also a center of the colonies' maritime resistance to the British in the Revolution. In the nineteenth century, great clipper ships were built here. Now Mystic is best known for the Marine Historical Museum which harbors the only surviving nineteenth-century whaler, the *Charles W Morgan.*

*Opposite:* Ocean Beach Park, south of the city of New London, lies at the mouth of the Thames River and is one of the many fine beaches along Connecticut's coast. New London is best known today as the home of the nation's Coast Guard Academy.

46

*Opposite:* A fine old eighteenth-century house — the Timothy Skinner House — is one of many still found in and around the historic town of Litchfield, in northwestern Connecticut.

*Left:* William Gillette, a popular actor early in this century, designed his medieval castle. Built in 1919 in Hadlyme, it is now part of a state park.

*Above:* Mark Twain had this house built for himself in 1874 on the edge of Hartford. He wrote many of his finest works while living here, but debts forced him to sell it in 1891. Now restored to its original condition and full of Twain's personal memorabilia, it is open to the public as a museum.

*Top left:* The Buttolph-Williams House, built by David Buttolph in 1692, is one of some 150 buildings still standing in Wethersfield that pre-date the mid-nineteenth century. Wethersfield is just south of Hartford.

*Top right:* The parlor of the Buttolph-Williams House, which along with a kitchen took up the ground floor, with two bedrooms on the second floor. The house was greatly altered in the eighteenth and nineteenth centuries, but it has now been restored and furnished with authentic period pieces. With its post-and-girt construction not far removed from medieval methods, this is one of the finest seventeenth-century houses in America.

# New Hampshire

# New Hampshire

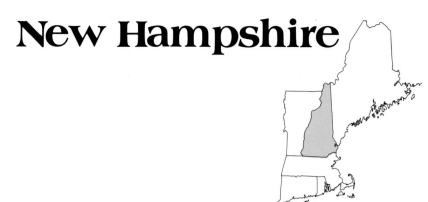

Since the mid-1900s, New Hampshire has become increasingly urban and industrialized, continuing the trend which began after the Civil War. But most of this urban activity is concentrated around Manchester, the state's largest city, and a surprising 90 percent of New Hampshire's land area remains covered with forest. The Granite State's 34 state parks, 103 state forests, historic sites and great natural beauty draw increasing numbers of visitors to its mountains and beaches for activities as diverse as skiing, yachting, dogsled racing, or simply gazing at the amazing fall foliage.

New Hampshire was first settled in 1623. John Mason named the region after his native county of Hampshire, England, when he was granted the territory in 1629 by the royal Council for New England. For a time New Hampshire became part of the Massachusetts Bay Colony, but it became a separate colony again under Charles II in 1680. With the rest of New England, New Hampshire suffered through the French and Indian War, then became increasingly disenchanted with the Mother Country during the 1760s because of oppressive taxes and trade restrictions. New Hampshirites figured prominently in the sack of Fort William and Mary, one of the first armed actions against the British, and on 5 January 1776 New Hampshire became the first colony to form a government wholly independent of England. On 21 June 1788, New Hampshire became the ninth state to ratify the US Constitution, completing the three-fourths majority necessary to put it into effect.

Today the pioneering spirit of democracy is still alive in New Hampshire's 222 self-governing towns. Nicknamed 'little republics,' their functioning under three selectmen elected by voters at town meetings is one of the purest forms of democracy in the world. Cities likewise exercise considerable home rule, and are free to amend their charters themselves. At the state level, instead of a lieutenant governor, New Hampshire has a five-man executive council which must approve executive officials appointed by the governor.

Granite is no longer an important product of the Granite State, but several of its other natural features rate superlatives. Its heavily wooded hills remain, in many areas, much as they were seen by the native Indians and the early settlers. Its many lakes and rivers provide an oasis of quiet and natural beauty in an increasingly urban world.

*Preceding pages:* Hardwood trees take on autumn colors in Conway, looking out over Mount Washington Valley. The town is a gateway to White Mountain skiing.

*Left:* Pittsfield, a lakeside village with the church steeple and white clapboard houses typical of so many small towns to be found in New Hampshire.

*Left:* Fishing on Profile Lake. New Hampshire's Lakes Region, in the southern part of the state centered around the community of Laconia, has been a favorite with visitors for generations. Primarily a summer resort area, its fishing and boating give way to skiing in winter.

*Below left:* Sailing on Lake Sunapee. Mount Sunapee State Park is one of 34 state parks in New Hampshire. In July and August New Hampshire's many lakes feature sailing regattas. Excursion boats leave from Sunapee Harbor all summer, and Sunapee is also a major ski area.

*Below:* Indians taught the Europeans to make maple syrup and sugar products by tapping maple trees in the spring. After the rising sap is collected in buckets, it must be carefully heated to concentrate the sweetness.

*Opposite:* The beautiful colors of fall foliage enliven the banks of a stream at Wildcat Mountain. Located in the Glen Ellis Falls Scenic Area and featuring the first enclosed gondola cable car in America, Wildcat is one of eight peaks in the White Mountain National Forest that tower over a mile above sea level.

*Preceding pages:* A placid, autumnal scene on the Swift River. Covered bridges grace many of New Hampshire's rivers and streams.
*Opposite:* 'Aspet,' the home of artist Augustus Saint-Gaudens, is now a National Historic Site.
*Top:* The Franklin Pierce Homestead in Hillsboro, the childhood home of New Hampshire's only president, was built in 1804.
*Above:* Strawbery Banke Museum in Portsmouth, the port to which Paul Revere rode on 13 December 1774. Strawbery Banke, Portsmouth's original name, is now a restored area featuring seventeenth- and eighteenth-century buildings and crafts.

*Preceding pages:* Mount Washington, the highest point in the northeastern United States, is the central peak of the White Mountains. Here the world's first cog railway was built in 1869. The highest wind speed ever observed, 231 mph, was recorded here on 12 April 1934.

*Above:* Woods near Lyme, north of Hanover close to the Connecticut River. Lyme was an important stagecoach stop between Boston and Montreal in the early years of the nineteenth century and has several period inns and houses.

*Above right:* Spring blossoms in Auburn on Massabesic Lake east of Manchester. New Hampshire is blessed with numerous lakes, rivers and streams, many of which were channeled into millponds and spillways such as this one to power the state's nineteenth-century industrialization.

*Right:* An ice sculpture at the Dartmouth Winter Carnival. Dartmouth College was established four years after the first white settlers came (1769) 'for the instruction of the Youth of Indian tribes . . . and others' and has since dominated the cultural life of Hanover.

*Opposite:* A winter scene in the village of Marlow, on the Asheulot River. Church, school, town hall and houses all in white framed by birches in the foreground and hills on the horizon offer ample illustration of the simple elegance that has drawn visitors for 200 years.

Vermont

# Vermont

Green Vermont—the French called it *Vert Mont* or *Green Mountain* — is still three-fourths covered by forests, and 70 percent of its population lives in rural areas, the lowest percentage of city dwellers of any state in America. Only Rutland and Burlington, which is the only city in the state with over 30,000 inhabitants, boast populations of over 20,000, and the capital of Montpelier contains only 10,000 souls.

The Green Mountains for which Vermont is named run the entire length of the state, dividing it into eastern and western sections. Manufacturing is Vermont's primary industry, but the beauty of the state's wilderness in all seasons has made tourism a close second. In 1911 Vermont became the first state to open a publicity bureau for the express purpose of attracting tourists.

French explorer Samuel de Champlain claimed Vermont for France in 1609. In 1724 the first permanent white settlement was built to warn western Massachusetts villages of Indian attacks, and in 1763 England gained control of the region. The Revolutionary War began for Vermont in 1775, when the Green Mountain Boys captured Fort Ticonderoga, across Lake Champlain. In 1777 Vermont declared itself an independent republic and became the first future state to include universal male suffrage in its constitution. After fourteen years as an independent nation, Vermont became the first state added to the thirteen original colonies. Annual town meetings, the basic unit of American democracy, are still the cornerstone of Vermont government.

In the late 1700s, 'Indian Sugar' made from maple syrup was an important Vermont commodity. More easily farmed land attracted many Vermonters to the Midwest in the early nineteenth century, but the Champlain Canal, which enabled Vermonters to ship by water directly to Manhattan, created a wool boom and prosperous conditions until the middle of the century. In 1840 Vermont had six times as many sheep as persons. When the wool market moved elsewhere, Vermont concentrated on dairy farming. Agriculture and mining, still more important to Vermont than to any other state, were eclipsed by tourism at the beginning of this century. Today Vermont seeks to attract more industry and tourism, but the state's environmental control law, passed in 1970, is evidence of the Green Mountain State's firm determination to maintain its unique rural character and keep its natural wonders intact.

*Preceding pages:* Autumn in Waits River, Orange County. The counties of Orleans and Essex — the Northeast Kingdom — are the least developed in Vermont.

*Opposite:* Cows graze on a Vermont hillside on a lazy summer afternoon. The population of people did not surpass that of cows in this state until the 1960's.

*Above:* The sun sets over hills west of Charlotte, into Lake Champlain. Vermont is the only New England state with neither coast nor shoreline, but vast Lake Champlain forms about half of its western border. A ferry runs from Charlotte across the lake to Essex, New York. Charlotte boasts excellent orchard country, and its Congregational church, over 100 years old, is one of the few Greek Revival structures in Vermont.

*Right:* Skiers make their way down a scenic slope in the Sugarbush Valley Ski Area in Warren. The Sugarbush Valley area has an elevation of more than 4000 feet. High-elevation snowmaking insures skiing from October to mid-May, and for summer enjoyment the resort offers golf, tennis and hiking.

*Opposite:* Five-mile-long Mount Mansfield, the highest peak in Vermont (4393 feet), has become famous for skiing and magnificent views. Stowe, one of Vermont's most sophisticated communities, and its ski areas, receive 120 inches or more of snow a year and attract visitors from all over the world. The Mt Mansfield Ski Club has done much to make American skiers international competitors.

*Opposite:* Burlington, 'Queen City of Vermont,' is the largest city in Vermont and the most important port on Lake Champlain. It is situated on a three-terraced slope at the widest point of the lake, facing the Adirondacks to the west and backed by Vermont's Green Mountains. Its tree-covered summit is occupied by residential districts and the University of Vermont, Vermont's oldest university; the middle terrace is occupied by some 72 industries employing over 24,000 people. Docks, shops and warehouses fit in below.

*Above:* Tyler Place, Lake Champlain, named after Royall Tyler (1757-1820), former chief justice of the Vermont Supreme Court and professor of jurisprudence at the University of Vermont, Burlington. Tyler wrote the first American comedy (*The Contrast,* 1786) to be regularly acted on a professional stage and wrote the first American novel (*The Algerine Captive,* 1797) to be published in England. Through characters in these works Tyler created the first real Yankee type found in literature.

71

*Preceding pages:* Illuminated by afternoon light, mountains create a warm backdrop to a chilly autumn scene in Pittsford.

*Opposite:* The Walter K Howe farm, near Tunbridge, backed by October foliage. In mid-September thousands of people from nearby counties gather for the century-old Tunbridge World's Fair.

*Above:* A Vermont dairy farm and maple-lined road represent two of Vermont's natural industries. Sugar maples also supply some of the best fall colors.

*Left:* A toadstool from the woods near Hancock, on the White River at the edge of Green Mountain National Forest. The mountains forests are filled with hidden beauties.

*Overleaf:* An exquisite winter scene near Barre, the center of Vermont's granite industry. The largest granite quarries in the United States are found near Barre.

The colors of Indian summer bathe farmland in Vermont's northwestern Franklin County, on the Canadian border.

Maine

# Maine

First explored by Viking sailors 1000 years ago and settled by Europeans before the Pilgrims arrived at Plymouth, the state of Maine has always gone its own way. In 1851 Maine, whose name is derived from *The Main* or *Mainland*, effectively banned the production and sale of alcoholic beverages almost 70 years before Prohibition became the law of the land. The same rugged coastline studded with coves, inlets, bays and islands which enticed early explorers and fostered Maine's important colonial shipbuilding industry — America's first ship was launched on the Kennebec River in 1607 — now attracts tourists. But almost every seacoast community still has at least a small fleet of fishing boats, and the interior, blessed with thousands of lakes, streams, mountains and 18 million acres of forests, still provides the raw materials that make wood-processing the mainstay of the Pine Tree State's economy. By far the largest state in New England, Maine each year supplies the rest of the country with more toothpicks (about 125 million) and more lobsters (about 18.5 million pounds) than any other state in the Union.

In 1641 York (then Gorgeana), Maine became the first chartered English city in what was to become the United States. Thirty-six years later, Maine was acquired by Massachusetts for about $6000, and remained part of the Bay State for the next 142 years. In 1775 the first naval battle of the Revolutionary War was fought off the coast of Maine, resulting in the capture of the British schooner *Margaretta*. In 1819 Maine voted to separate from Massachusetts, and in 1820 it was admitted to the Union, becoming the twenty-third and easternmost state. Long-standing boundary disputes with Canada, resulting in the so-called Aroostook War of 1839, were finally settled by the Webster-Ashburton Treaty of 1842.

Augusta has been the capital since 1842, but Portland is now by far the largest city and the only one with a population of over 30,000. The stunning Acadia National Park on Mount Desert Island, preserving Maine as it was when the first Europeans arrived, is the only national park in New England; and the Portland Head Light, built in 1791 by order of President George Washington, and towering 101 feet above the surf, is one of the oldest and most famous lighthouses in the United States. Today Maine still makes its living between its forests and its seas, and whether it continues to do so primarily from the products of these vast resources, or from the millions of visitors who come to see them, the Pine Tree State is certain to go its own way, supported by its natural wonders, for the foreseeable future.

*Preceding pages:* A house along the rugged coast at Kennebunkport. This town on Maine's southern coast is a summer resort as well as an arts colony.

*Opposite:* Pemaquid Point Light, one of the famous lighthouses which dot Maine's rocky coast. A Viking skeleton dressed in armor was found nearby in 1965.

*Left:* Lobstermen at work. Each year Maine supplies about 18.5 million pounds of lobster to the rest of America, more than any other state. Lobsters, like turtles, live hundreds of years and continue to grow, but can only be taken when their main shell reaches a certain length.

*Lower left:* A seagull eyes the scenery at Cape Elizabeth, one of the most awe-inspiring shorelines in Maine. Many visit here after a storm to watch the surf pound against the jumbled rock. The painter Winslow Homer lived nearby, and President Washington ordered neighboring Portland Head Light, which is visible on clear days, into commission in 1791.

*Lower right:* A seafood festival at Bar Harbor, the largest town on Mount Desert Island. The island includes most of Acadia National Park.

*Right:* Lobster buoys in Bernard. Each lobster fisherman creates his own unique color code for the buoys which indicate the location of his traps, or 'pots.' Taking lobsters from another's pots is subject to severe legal penalties, and sometimes to vigilante actions, for unless a buoy breaks adrift a man's pots are always distinguishable, and the lobstering industry is based on mutual trust.

*Opposite:* Black Cove in New Harbor is typical of hundreds of lobstering villages to be found along the Maine coast. Almost no seacoast town is without its small fishing fleet, fishing shacks and stacks of pots.

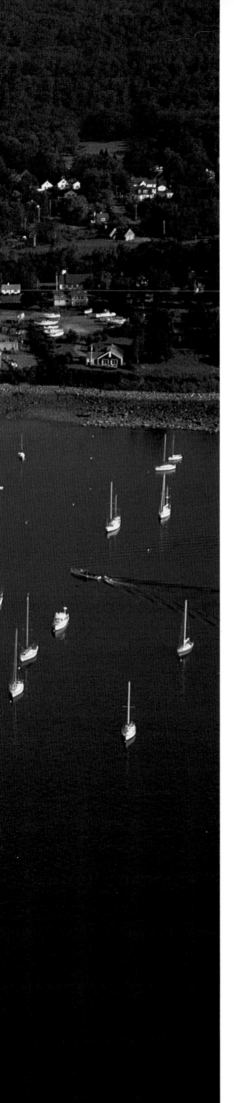

*Opposite:* Camden, in Maine's Penobscot region, is one of the loveliest coastal resort areas to be found in Maine or anywhere else. A popular yachting center with breathtaking long-distance views of Penobscot Bay and its many islands, the town, under which the Camden River runs before cascading into the harbor, is a delightful place to wander on foot. Musicians and music lovers can take advantage of the musical programs at the outdoor Amphitheater.

*Above:* Camden is the preeminent port for Maine windjammer cruises. The schooners *Mattie* and *Mercantile* are available for week-long cruises, and there are boats which cruise to nearby islands for the day. On shore, the Camden Hills rise abruptly from Penobscot Bay, a unique physical feature. The 1.4-mile summit of Mount Battie provides a breathtaking panoramic view of the bay, the islands and the peninsulas beyond.

*Above:* Monhegan Island, nine miles out to sea, two miles long and one mile wide, has a summer population 20 times the year-round number. Most natives are lobster fishermen who take the premium-priced Monhegan lobsters from local waters from January to June.

*Below:* One of the many small islands— some inhabited, some uninhabited— which dot the Maine coastal waters. From earliest times Maine's many islands and rugged coast fascinated explorers. Leif Ericson landed on Monhegan in AD 1000.

*Opposite:* Yachting is the main attraction at Northeast Harbor, one of the coastal villages of Mount Desert Island. Summer residents and visiting yachtsmen gather by the hundreds in boats of every shape and size for regattas, races and cruises.

*Opposite:* 'Down home' Maine is just like it seems: pretty without being prettified.
*Above:* The Indians were paid twenty beaver pelts for the Boothbays, an intricate network of islands, coves, rivers, peninsulas and harbors of which Boothbay Harbor is the centerpiece. Pictured here is the fishing village and summer resort of East Boothbay, with its white Congregational church.

*Overleaf:* Camden, one of Maine's most popular coastal resorts, with its windjammers put away for winter storage.
*Pages 94 & 95:* Further up the peninsula but not entirely free from the influence of bays and inlets is the classic village of Sheepscot.
*Page 96:* Just north of York beach is Cape Neddick, picturesque 'Nubble Light,' and an exquisite view of the northward-reaching coast.